Remembering
Fort Lauderdale

Susan Gillis

TURNER
PUBLISHING COMPANY

This view shows the crowded "strip," the main drag of Fort Lauderdale's extensive beachfront in 1937. The city fought from its early days to discourage private ownership of beachfront property and to maintain a public beach and right-of-way for its citizens.

Remembering
Fort Lauderdale

Turner Publishing Company
4507 Charlotte Avenue • Suite 100
Nashville, Tennessee 37209
(615) 255-2665

Remembering Fort Lauderdale

www.turnerpublishing.com

Copyright © 2010 Turner Publishing Company

Library of Congress Control Number: 2010924313

ISBN: 978-1-59652-656-3

Printed in the United States of America

ISBN: 978-1-68336-830-4 (pbk)

10 11 12 13 14 15 16—0 9 8 7 6 5 4 3 2 1

CONTENTS

In 1937, the construction of the Lauderdale Beach Hotel, shown at the center of the photo, signaled a new era of tourism for Fort Lauderdale. At far-left, the floating hotel Amphitrite is visible on the old Las Olas Causeway in this photo taken about 1939. The Nurmi Isles in the background remain to be developed in this image.

ACKNOWLEDGMENTS

This volume, *Remembering Fort Lauderdale,* is the result of the cooperation and efforts of many individuals and organizations. It is with great thanks that we acknowledge the valuable contribution of the following for their generous support:

Broward County Historical Commission
Fort Lauderdale Historical Society
State Library and Archives of Florida

The writer would like to thank Ms. Denyse Cunningham of the Broward County Historical Commission for her invaluable assistance with this project. This volume would not have been possible without the extensive research collections of the Historical Commission and the Fort Lauderdale Historical Society.

———————

The goal in publishing this work is to provide broader access to a set of extraordinary photographs. The aim is to inspire, provide perspective, and evoke insight that might assist officials and citizens, who together are responsible for determining Fort Lauderdale's future. In addition, the book seeks to preserve the past with respect and reverence.

With the exception of cropping where necessary and touching up imperfections wrought by time, no other changes have been made. The focus and clarity of many images is limited to the technology of the day and the skill of the photographer who captured them.

—*Todd Bottorff, Publisher*

PREFACE

No one knows for sure the origins of New River's name. The Rio Novo first appeared on Spanish maps by the seventeenth century. For thousands of years, people have called the picturesque New River home. The ancient Tequesta Indians of South Florida once plied its waters in their dugouts; they had all left South Florida by the end of the eighteenth century.

In the 1790s, new pioneers arrived along New River and a small settlement began to grow up there. Bahamians who survived by farming and wrecking (salvaging) were joined by Americans when Florida became a territory in 1821. The Seminole Indians, originally from tribes whites collectively called "Creeks," had made their way from Georgia and the Carolinas into South Florida by this time as well—and conflict soon ensued.

In December 1835, the Second Seminole War broke out. In January, the family of local justice of the peace William Cooley was killed by a group of Indians while Cooley and others were away salvaging a shipwreck. In March of 1838, Major William Lauderdale and his Tennessee Volunteers, with Robert Anderson and Company D, Third U.S. Artillery, came to New River. They established an encampment at the forks of the river and named it Fort Lauderdale, in honor of the ranking officer. There were three Fort Lauderdales during the war years; the third and most permanent was located at the beach where Bahia Mar is now.

The years after the Second and Third Seminole Wars were quiet ones on New River. A few intrepid souls called the wilderness home. In 1893 a stageline was established on the new Dade County Road, which stretched from Lantana (now Palm Beach County) to Lemon City (now North Miami). Ohioan Frank Stranahan came to New River to operate a ferry and overnight camp for the stage. He decided to open a store as well, a welcome center for trade with the local Indians. Instead of "New River," he named it "Fort Lauderdale" in honor of events that seemed, even then, a part of the distant past. From this humble origin a new town grew. By 1896, Henry Flagler's Florida East Coast Railway began through-service to Miami and "civilization" began in earnest. The tropical wilderness would never be the same.

It is here, just after the turn of the century, that our story begins. The images in this book are divided into four sections. The first section, spanning the 1910s, examines the growth of the community into a riverport town. Stranahan's trading post, the coming of the railway, and the establishment of the Everglades drainage canals all came within a few short years and resulted in the 1911 incorporation of the town of Fort Lauderdale.

The 1920s and 1930s were the eras of "boom and bust" for South Floridians. Fort Lauderdale was at the very heart of the 1920s land boom, and urbanization began in earnest. Tourism and real estate were in; farming was relegated to the hinterlands of the county. Two killer hurricanes, one in 1926 and one in 1928, put the final cap on the boom times, but Fort Lauderdale residents rebuilt their community and kept going through belt-tightening times, confident that the lure of the beach and climate would continue to attract the almighty tourist dollar.

Section Three examines the 1940s and 1950s through war and peace. Fort Lauderdale played host to a number of military installations, and citizens supported the war effort with bond drives, blackouts, and rationing. The winter of 1945-46 was the best tourist season for the city up to that time. The ensuing years saw another boom for the area as thousands of former servicemen returned, this time with their families, to settle in the land they had grown fond of during the war.

During the 1960s and 1970s, Fort Lauderdale became Florida's "fastest-growing city." New developments filled the city limits while high-rise co-ops and condominiums began to grow up along the skyline. Fort Lauderdale earned its hard-to-shake sobriquet "Where the Boys Are," for its Spring Break crowds. National issues like civil rights and the Cold War had a direct impact on local citizens; life was changing in what had been a small town in the South. By the end of the 1970s, Fort Lauderdale had almost reached build-out, hemmed in by other growing municipalities within the county, but it continued to serve as the social, political, and governmental center of Broward County—and still does so today.

—*Susan Gillis*

The completion of the Florida East Coast Railway from West Palm Beach to Miami was a pivotal event in the history of South Florida. It brought settlers and supplies and provided a much-needed transportation route for agricultural products such as winter vegetables. The first passenger train arrived in the little settlement of Fort Lauderdale on February 11, 1896. In April, through-service began to Miami, and South Florida was a wilderness no more.

A New Town

(1900s–1919)

Few of us can imagine the challenges that faced the settlers of the young community of Fort Lauderdale at the turn of the century. The sometimes oppressive heat and numerous pests would have daunted many pioneers, but the warm winter climate, endless waterways, and tropical scenery attracted others. Here several of the townsfolk have gathered for a picnic, in fashionable regalia, on New River about 1909.

Fort Lauderdale's downtown was virtually destroyed by fire on June 1, 1912. The town council responded by establishing a volunteer fire department and initiating water and sewer service for the newly incorporated community. This view shows Brickell Avenue, facing toward the northeast, from a vantage above New River—probably atop the Florida East Coast Railway bridge.

On July 17, 1913, the last survivor of the 1912 downtown fire itself ironically succumbed to fire. The Osceola Hotel was a three-story, wood-frame structure originally constructed as a warehouse and later converted to a hostelry to house the many new investors and settlers coming to the area. This north-facing view shows the new fire department in action on Brickell Avenue.

The British-born "Commodore" A. H. Brook arrived in Fort Lauderdale in 1919 and immediately became one of its principal boosters and a renowned activist. He made his home in the historic neighborhood of Sailboat Bend, located on New River just west of downtown. This photograph shows the fine river view from his home, Brookside, with his sailboat, *Klyo,* moored at center.

With the completion of the North New River Canal in 1912, it was possible to travel from Fort Lauderdale to Fort Myers inland by water. South Florida enjoyed its very own steamboat era as boats brought prospective land buyers and growers' crops back and forth from Lake Okeechobee to the railhead at Fort Lauderdale. Pioneer Ivan Austin photographed this scene along the canal in 1913.

This rare interior view shows the new county's prosecuting attorney Gregers A. Frost in his courthouse office in 1915. County commission meetings were often held in this office in the first days of county government. The frontier town of Fort Lauderdale had acquired telephone and electric service by this time, evidenced by the phone to the left and light fixture to the right of attorney Frost.

On June 15, 1915, the White Star bus line began operations between Palm Beach and Miami. The open-sided buses, named for the manufacturer (White) were actually owned by Fort Lauderdalians. Two buses each made a complete run once a day. The White Star Line was later sold to the Greyhound Bus company. Here, travelers enjoy a beautiful tropical vista along the roadway—a far cry from today's interstate.

Famous director D. W. Griffith oversees a location shot on New River in 1919. Pioneer camera artist "Billy" Blitzer stands at left. Fort Lauderdale briefly became a movie capital during the late 1910s and early 1920s, as its unspoiled tropical scenery attracted directors.

In 1917, the Las Olas Causeway was completed, at last linking Fort Lauderdale's beach area with downtown. A trip to the beach no longer relied on an available boat; it was much easier to hitch a ride on someone's "flivver." The beach and causeway encouraged an important industry in Fort Lauderdale: tourism. This photo features a joyful crowd in the late 1910s.

This wide-angle view shows Annie Jumper Tommie's compound located on what is now Broward Boulevard just east of I-95. Visible are the native pines and saw palmettos which once constituted the natural "landscaping" of Fort Lauderdale. The structures known as "chickees," made of cypress logs and palm thatch roofs, represented one of the Seminoles' creative adaptations to the South Florida climate.

Norwegian-born Sigurd Dillevig was a pattern maker at a Chicago foundry when a local firm selling Florida lands lured him to South Florida in 1912. Dillevig owned the town's only "marine ways," or marine railway, located on the point between the forks of New River. He also served in the Fort Lauderdale Home Guard, as can be seen in this photograph from about 1917.

Sam and Ethel Williams moved with their daughter Oleta to a small wooden house on the north fork of New River in 1916. Located in the rustic area then called the "west side"—today the neighborhood of Sailboat Bend—the house had no well or cistern when the Williams's moved there. The appeal of their suburban location is clear in this image, showing the pristine north fork of New River, looking down river (east) about 1917.

This view of North Andrews Avenue, facing north from the New River bridge, shows a patriotic parade around 1920. The new decade signaled truly a new era—agriculture and shipping no longer reigned supreme. Tourism and real estate became the new focus of the local economy. The Mediterranean-style Broward Hotel rises majestically in the center of the photograph.

Boom and Bust

(1920–1939)

Fort Lauderdale's first municipal band was organized in 1913 under the leadership of Glenn "Pop" Bates. The band provided a much-needed cultural respite for hard-working citizens, with concerts held on the riverfront on Brickell Avenue every Saturday night. Bates' wife, son, and two brothers played in the band, despite brother Beryl's missing arm. (He's third from the left, front row.) This photograph shows band members from the 1920-21 season.

One of Fort Lauderdale's most recognizable characters in the 1910s and 1920s was "Shirttail Charlie," a Seminole Indian who panhandled on the streets for a living. A legend grew that Shirttail had murdered his wife and been condemned to wear a woman's dress as punishment. The truth was he simply continued to wear the "big shirt" style, which was slowly being replaced by trousers and jackets among Seminole men.

On February 26, 1927, a group of Masons met to establish a local Shrine Club in Fort Lauderdale. Their charter was issued under the auspices of the Mahi Temple in Miami in May of that year. In July 1928, the club was granted permission to form an "Oriental Band." Here, band members, in regalia, are shown posing with their wives, who played a significant "supporting role" in all of the band's performances.

In 1921, local boosters Commodore Brook and Tom Stilwell "rescued" president-elect Warren G. Harding as he was traveling down the Intracoastal Waterway and met a grounded dredge mysteriously blocking the way. It was all part of an effort to promote the young city. Harding was a willing participant, even playing a round of golf. He is the dapper man in the black suit at center, posing with locals on the docks near the Andrews Avenue bridge.

In the days when radio was new and television unheard of, local baseball games were an engaging pastime in small-town America. Everyone turned out for the games of the Fort Lauderdale town team, shown here in 1921. They played teams from various neighboring communities, but "Beat Miami" was their rallying cry. Games were played on Stranahan Field, a site at the southwest corner of Federal Highway and Broward Boulevard.

The completion of the 1917 Las Olas Causeway resulted in the slow but steady development of Fort Lauderdale's now-famous beachfront. The cars lining what was then known as Las Olas Beach are a testament to its new-found popularity and the growing tourism industry. The north-facing view was photographed from the roof of the first Fort Lauderdale beach casino in 1925.

Pioneer Jimmy Vreeland, son of a onetime keeper of the House of Refuge—a rescue station and shelter for shipwrecked sailors, operated by the U.S. Life-Saving Service, the forerunner of the Coast Guard—became Fort Lauderdale's first charter boat captain. "Cap" Vreeland and his *Kingfisher* boats operated out of his private dock off Las Olas Boulevard, just east of the present causeway. This image features happy visitors with their catch on Vreeland's dock in the mid-1920s. The grouper at upper-left has a well-placed mackerel in its mouth.

Maypole dances were popular public entertainments held on the first of May at schools throughout America in the early twentieth century. In this photo, well-dressed students, probably likely from Central (later called Fort Lauderdale) High School, stand ready for the maypole dance in the early 1920s.

Fishing was a pleasurable and inexpensive pastime for locals as well as tourists in the 1920s. Fish of all varieties were extremely plentiful in the river, canals, and nearby Everglades, as well as the ocean. In this photo, "Dad" Sullivan poses with George Gillespie and Mary Louise Sullivan with a nice catch of mackerels in the mid-1920s.

Fort Lauderdale's volunteer fire department poses just outside the station's 1921 location, on what is today Southwest Second Street at Andrews Avenue. The building at left housed the town's first newspaper, the Fort Lauderdale *Sentinel*. The empty lots in the background belie the amazing growth of Andrews Avenue within the five years to come. The sign at right points to the road to the Everglades and a Seminole Indian camp attraction.

In 1925, at the height of the Florida land boom, Chicago salesman Frank Croissant came to Fort Lauderdale offering land for sale south of New River. Among the promotions for the new development of Croissant Park was a beauty contest. The swimsuit competition is shown here.

In 1913, pioneer entrepreneur Tom Bryan established the Fort Lauderdale Light and Ice Company in a building on Northwest Second Avenue. The power system was necessary to generate the ice; excess electricity could be sold to the public. By 1925, the "ice plant," was bought out by the young company Florida Power & Light, today South Florida's principal electric utility. This scene shows the FPL plant on September 7, 1926.

Andrews Avenue had supplanted Brickell as the city's main street by the mid-1920s. This view shows the proliferation of new commercial structures that arose within a few years during the height of the Florida land boom. Notice the one-way traffic and the city's first skyscraper, the Sweet Building, under construction in the background at right.

On September 18, 1926, a Category Four hurricane brought the crushing final blow to the Florida boom. The devastation in Fort Lauderdale was spectacular. This view of the Maxwell Arcade shows the damage to an electric sign reportedly built at the amazing cost of $150,000. The building, however, survives today on the southeast side of the Andrews Avenue bridge.

The 1926 storm affected South Floridians from southern Dade County to as far north as Lake Okeechobee, causing at least 240 deaths and $159 million in damages—well over a billion dollars in today's currency. This image shows the Ford garage in Fort Lauderdale, which lost its entire second floor. The dramatic image by Hollywood photographer H. G. Higby was used in a number of contemporary publications documenting the storm damage.

Until 1927 only one rail line extended into South Florida, Henry Flagler's FEC Railway. On January 8, 1927, locals at Fort Lauderdale greet the much-anticipated arrival of the "Orange Blossom Special," the new train of the Seaboard Air Line Railway. One of the attendees was Dorothy Walker Bush (in the floral dress at right), mother of future president George H. W. Bush.

Merle Fogg was killed in a plane crash on May 1, 1928. When city fathers decided to convert the Southside Golf Course into an airfield, it was named in his honor. Merle Fogg Field was dedicated in 1929. The modest field became the Fort Lauderdale Naval Air Station during World War II. Today, it is the Fort Lauderdale Hollywood International Airport.

By the 1930s, Fort Lauderdale's African-American community had established a separate business district west of the FEC tracks and north of Broward Boulevard. One of the success stories of the era was "T. S." Cobb, owner of the Bedd-O-Rest Company, which manufactured mattresses, sofas, and draperies. Here Cobb and an employee pose in their booth at the county fair in 1935.

Despite the onset of the Great Depression, new technology held the same appeal for Fort Lauderdale residents in the 1930s as it does today. In this wonderful shot of the interior of the Florida Power & Light Company office in 1931, fine, new electrical appliances such as the latest washing machine, stove, and other gadgets lure the prospective buyer. Edison light bulbs fill two shelves and a table display.

The Ullian family first came to Fort Lauderdale in the late 1920s. Second-generation Alfred and Helen Shapiro Ullian resided at the southeast corner of Southeast Sixth Street and Andrews Avenue during the 1930s. In this charming photo from 1934, their daughter Norma poses on a goat cart outside what is probably the family home.

The 1930s proved to be hard times for the local Seminoles. The Everglades drainage canals had forever altered their water-reliant lifestyle, and jobs were in short supply for all citizens. Many Seminoles continued to make their home in the wilds of the Everglades. In this photograph taken for Indian agent James Glenn in 1935, a woman hangs hog meat to dry at a typical Seminole camp.

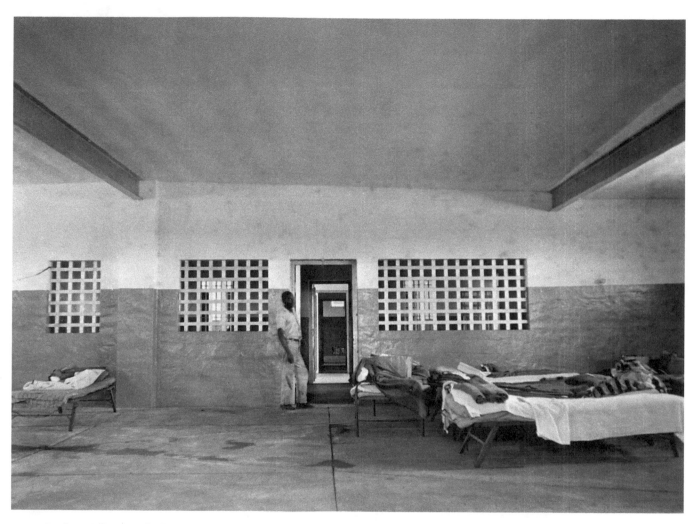

In the 1930s, sheriffs throughout Florida routinely rounded up African-Americans on vagrancy charges during harvest time, whereupon they had to work off the fine in the farm fields. Sheriff Walter Clark and his brother Deputy Sheriff Robert Clark were paid by local farmers for the use of the prison labor. Home for the "workers" was the Broward County Prison Camp, located on Northeast Thirteenth Street at Seventeenth Avenue. A typical dorm room is shown here in 1935.

The Federal Emergency Relief Agency, one of the "alphabet agencies" of the Great Depression, was organized through tax dollars to provide relief to the unemployed in America. A key goal was to train women in marketable skills, making it possible for them to supplement their income. In this image from 1935, Fort Lauderdale women learn to make basketry using local materials.

One of the FERA projects was the construction of a scouting camp on the wilds of Middle River, at the northern limits of Fort Lauderdale. Here local boy scouts conduct a fire-making contest at the camp in 1935. Native pines—long gone now—are visible in the background.

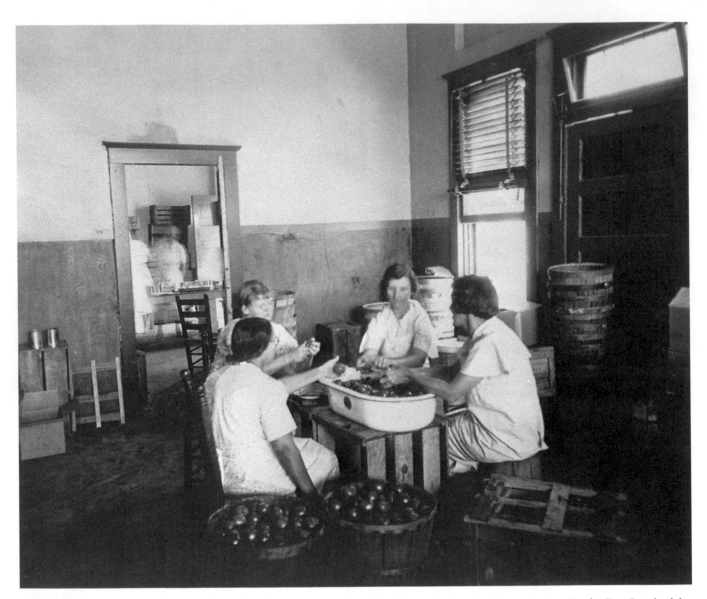

The Federal Emergency Relief Agency taught urban women to be self-sufficient during the Depression era. In the Fort Lauderdale area, four canning kitchens trained local women in food preservation techniques. Here women prepare tomatoes for canning in 1935. Tomatoes had long been one of Broward County's most popular crops, easily grown and easily transported to northern markets. The Dania area, for example, was known as the "tomato capital" until well into the 1950s. Salt-water intrusion into local soils finally ended local tomato production.

Port Everglades, Fort Lauderdale's deepwater harbor, officially opened in 1928. The 1930s saw the maturing of the port and the arrival of the first cruise ship, the SS *Columbia,* which paid its first visit on January 18, 1932.

The *Amphitrite* was a monitor-class naval vessel brought to Fort Lauderdale in 1931 and converted to serve as a novel floating hotel. Originally docked to the west of the Coast Guard base, it was blown to the shores of neighboring Idlewyld during the 1935 hurricane. It was then relocated to the "mole" at the center of the Las Olas Causeway, where it is shown in this image.

President Franklin Delano Roosevelt visited Fort Lauderdale on a number of occasions during his terms in office, generally on his way to board his yacht *Potomac* for a bit of fishing R and R. In this photograph, he is boarding the Navy destroyer *Monaghan* at Port Everglades on March 23, 1936.

Sears Roebuck opened its new store at 101–103 South Andrews Avenue in January 1937. It was the only Sears store of its class to boast air conditioning and elevator service. Sears departed downtown for fine, new digs at "Searstown" on North Federal Highway in 1955. This view shows the Sears store and Andrews Avenue, looking south from Broward Boulevard in the late 1930s.

One of Fort Lauderdale's most famous citizens was Katherine "Katy" Rawls, well-known by her classmates at Fort Lauderdale High for her amazing athletic abilities. A champion swimmer and diver, she brought home silver and bronze medals in swimming and diving from the 1936 Olympics. In 1937, she was chosen Female Athlete of the Year by the Associated Press.

The 1930s were hard times for citizens of Fort Lauderdale. Despite the depression, former mayor Thomas Manuel recalled, "We had a great belief in the future because we knew as long as we had the sun and the ocean that people were going to come here . . . and they did." Here visitors and locals alike find inexpensive recreation along Fort Lauderdale's south beach in the late 1930s.

In 1936, the Works Progress Administration constructed a new main post office for Fort Lauderdale on Southeast First Avenue at Southeast Second Street. It drew businesses and eateries to the adjacent streets, just a block away from Andrews Avenue. The post office was demolished in 1974, and the city parking garage now stands on the site.

In 1933, the Prohibition amendment was finally repealed, ending an interesting era of rum-running and illicit saloons in South Florida. Repeal also encouraged the construction of legal establishments like the swanky, Art Deco 700 Club, shown here in 1937. The club operated at 700 East Las Olas Boulevard until 1954.

Soon after Port Everglades was opened in 1928, locals recognized the need for rail access to and from the port. In 1931, the Port Everglades Belt Railway was completed to link the port with the FEC and SAL line. This image shows belt railway engine Number 201 on February 26, 1938.

One of Fort Lauderdale's best-known citizens of the 1930s was County Sheriff Walter Clark (left). Known for his generosity and fairness in some quarters he was also hated and feared by many in the African-American community. Here Clark, with FBI agents Joe Conderman (center) and R. L. Shivers (right), examine jewels recovered from a stash found in an African-American cemetery in Hollywood in 1938.

Fort Lauderdale's premier convention hotel was the Governors' Club, located on Las Olas Boulevard, a few blocks west of Andrews Avenue. Originally begun as the "Wil Mar" hotel during the boom of the 1920s, the structure sat as an uncompleted shell until finished by Fort Lauderdale *News* owner R. H. Gore in 1937. It was named in honor of Gore's brief tenure as governor of Puerto Rico.

This photograph, shot looking north from the Andrews Avenue bridge in March 1939, shows that downtown remains much the same as in the 1920s, with the addition of a number of "modernizing" features like the black-and-white Art-Moderne-style tile work on the building at left. The tall building at left is the Sweet Building, which still stands as One River Plaza. All of the other structures visible in the image are long gone.

This view recorded by G. W. Romer in 1939 from the Sweet Building shows Fort Lauderdale's New River and the Andrews Avenue bridge. In the left background is the rear of the 1928 Broward County Courthouse. On the opposite side of the river are the twin structures of the Maxwell Arcade, which still stand today. The 1979 bascule bridge, with its much larger drawspan, completely altered this view and made inaccessible the streets next to the river, North and South New River Drive.

The Fort Lauderdale Golf & Country Club, also known as the "Westside Golf Course," was constructed in 1926 west of State Road 7 on Broward Boulevard, well west of town. The beautiful Mediterranean-style structure was designed by local architect Francis Abreu. Westside served as the city's only course until 1957, when the city commission put the club up for sale rather than face integration. This image shows the clubhouse about 1940.

THE VENICE OF AMERICA

(1940–1959)

Walter Reid Clark, one of the first people born in the city of Fort Lauderdale, served as Broward County sheriff from 1933 through 1950. Clark tolerated the illegal casinos and gambling operations within the county during his tenure; in return he controlled bolita and the local slot machines. In 1950, he was indicted by the Kefauver Commission on national television for his knowledge of illegal activities. Clark died in 1951, soon after his acquittal for possession of slot machines.

By 1942, Fort Lauderdale was quickly becoming an armed camp with a naval air station, Navy section base, Coast Artillery, and Coast Guard installations opening for business. In this photo, the Fort Lauderdale Home Guard drills outside the Fort Lauderdale City Hall and fire station, located on South Andrews Avenue just north of Second Street. Today, this is the site of the Broward Government Center. The guardsmen are wearing M1917/M1917A1 helmets; the soon-to-be famous M1 "steel pot" replacement design had only been adopted for U.S. troops the previous year.

During the war, the Fort Lauderdale's Service Men's Center, a recreation center sponsored by the local community, brought together thousands of visiting servicemen with local girls. Here future husband and wife R. L. Landers and Helen Herriott, the couple at right, escape the beach crowds by finding a spot on the private Bonnet House beach, just south of today's Sunrise Boulevard.

The war bond program provided not only economic support for the war effort but a patriotic rallying point as well. War bonds were sold at all sorts of local establishments like area theaters, shown here. In this image, the "Bond Belle" urges people to remember Sandy Nininger, Fort Lauderdale's first Congressional Medal of Honor winner, who was killed at Bataan early in 1942.

The Japanese surrender in August 1945 brought spontaneous celebrations throughout the city of Fort Lauderdale. Local citizens awaited the return of friends and family, while the thousands of servicemen in residence realized they would soon be returning home. Here a group of sailors and a couple of newsboys enjoy one of the Miami *Herald*'s most impressive headlines.

The winter of 1945-46 proved to be the city's most successful tourist season to date as travel restrictions were lifted, blackouts ended, and rationing forgotten. This classic scene shows visitors on Fort Lauderdale's beach in 1946.

Downtown Fort Lauderdale is booming in this view looking north from Las Olas Boulevard on Andrews Avenue in the 1940s. In the 1980s, the intersection of East Las Olas Boulevard and Andrews, shown at right, was jogged to the north to accommodate the wider approach of the current bridge over New River.

Boat parades and regattas have been a staple of Fort Lauderdale life since its earliest days. This ketch on New River seems to advertise such an event in 1946.

Two young ladies, displaying the latest in 1940s resort wear, do a bit of sunbathing on Fort Lauderdale's beach in 1946. The grande dame of the beach, the Lauderdale Beach Hotel, appears in the background at left.

Tourists, like the indolent sun worshipers shown here, arrived in Fort Lauderdale by the thousands in the winter of 1946. One newspaper headline claimed, "Fort Lauderdale swamped by 65,000." Historians August Burghard and Phil Weidling recalled, "Never had so many people with so much money descended upon Fort Lauderdale."

The old school building on South Andrews Avenue, which had served as the first county courthouse, by the late 1940s saw service as the home of the county health department. Citizens lined up to receive typhoid shots after the Flood of 1947 caused serious concerns about the possibility of an outbreak.

This aerial view by photographer Sherman Fairchild displays the growing community of Fort Lauderdale soon after World War II. New River can be seen at lower-right. The Florida East Coast Railway tracks are easily recognizable at the lower portion of the photo. The growing neighborhood of Victoria Park is visible at upper-left and the islands off Las Olas—cleared for development—at far-right.

Fulgencio Batista served as Cuba's president during the early 1940s and returned to power in a 1952 coup as a dictator friendly to the U.S. Batista, who called Daytona Beach his second home, had Broward County connections—such as mobster and gambling mogul Meyer Lansky. Batista is shown smiling, at right, next to Broward County Sheriff Clark in this photo by Steve Cresse, taken around 1950.

By the 1940s, eager tourists could travel to South Florida aboard the Seaboard Air Line's Silver Meteor, the deluxe New York–to–Miami passenger train. In 1967, the SAL merged with the Atlantic Coast Line to become the Seaboard Coast Line, or SCL. The Seaboard tracks eventually became the route of the U.S. government train service, Amtrak. Here a train chugs south out of the Fort Lauderdale station in 1947.

Scouting was a very popular outlet for young men at midcentury. It provided an opportunity to learn practical skills, serve the community, make friends, and of course, have fun. Fort Lauderdale Kiwanis Club president Charles Armstrong and Kiwanis Scout Master Bill Hatlem greet Boy Scouts of America Troop 7 members Oliver Lovedahl and Russell Carlisle in this 1948 photograph.

Coast Guard Base 6 was commissioned on the southernmost part of Fort Lauderdale beach in 1924. After World War II, the property was acquired by the city for a new marina: Bahia Mar. This photo shows one of the buildings of the old base as construction on Bahia Mar begins in 1949.

The Blount Building, with its then-trendy International Style architecture, opened in 1940 on East Las Olas at Southeast First Avenue. It was the home of many of Fort Lauderdale's physicians and other professionals. It was demolished in 1973 as part of the city's massive downtown redevelopment project.

In 1937, the City of Fort Lauderdale acquired the old Granada Apartments on South Andrews Avenue. The remodeled structure opened as Broward General Hospital in 1938. This image shows the hospital in 1949. Today, this is the expansive complex known as Broward General Medical Center.

Fort Lauderdale's beautiful beach has played host to Easter Sunday services for decades. In this photo, the Salvation Army band plays before a crowd gathered for the sunrise service in 1950. The band is seated on the boardwalk, which once stood on the beach in front of the Lauderdale Beach Hotel.

Despite Fort Lauderdale's rapid urbanization at midcentury, there was still room for pleasurable rural activities like horseback riding at the edges of the city and in nearby rural towns like Davie. Here a young equestrian takes a turn around the paddock in 1950.

During the post–World War II boom, thousands of new residents were drawn to Fort Lauderdale by the sunny climate and economic opportunities to be had there. One of the principal draws was the extensive canal systems that provided "ocean access" for many homeowners living in relatively modest neighborhoods. This view depicts an idyllic Fort Lauderdale home (and boat) on a canal off Las Olas Boulevard in 1950.

Fort Lauderdale's finest example of what is known as the Art Moderne style is the Lauderdale Beach Hotel, which originally opened in 1937, signaling a new era in local tourism. This view shows the hotel in 1950; a boardwalk once graced the beachfront there. Today the building has been restored and adapted as high-end condos.

The Tropicanza Festival was a citywide event sponsored by the Chamber of Commerce to benefit a variety of local agencies and encourage springtime tourism in 1950. The weeklong festival included fishing tournaments, youth activities, a water show, a prize fight, and of course, a downtown parade. In this photo, Tropicanza Queen Betty McCall poses with her court on April 10, 1950.

In honor of Florida's heritage, the city's Tropicanza Festival had a vaguely Spanish and Caribbean theme. Fashion shows, carnivals, parades, and dances gave ladies a chance to show off their costumes. Here two professional models dressed as "senoritas" beckon guests to festival activities in April 1950.

One of the highlights of the Tropicanza Festival was the "masked ball" held at the Broward Hotel on the night of April 10, 1950. "Authentic Spanish costume" was the preferred attire, but the gentlemen in this picture seem to have largely ignored the dictum.

This idyllic scene, part of the Florida Department of Commerce's collection, depicts a family enjoying a "typical" backyard scene, Fort Lauderdale style, in the 1950s. Mom and Dad actually have their own personal cabana, at right, and the kids enjoy what was once the *de rigueur* accessory for Florida lawns—an umbrella table.

The family residing in this home along one of the city's many waterways in the 1950s has a cabin cruiser tied up to their dock. In addition to personal boats, waterfront owners often rented dock space to seasonal visitors. A friend in a small sailboat, just the right size for getting around the canals and river, is departing, at right.

One of Fort Lauderdale's best-known citizens at midcentury was Dwight L. Rogers. As a state representative, he sponsored the Homestead Exemption Act, from which all Florida homeowners benefit today. He was the first Fort Lauderdale resident to serve as a U.S. Congressman, elected in 1944. In this photo, he speaks at the dedication of Pepper Park in Fort Pierce, 1950.

Saint Anthony Parish, established in 1921, is the oldest Catholic parish in Broward County. In 1947, Chicago architects Barry and Kay designed a new church for Saint Anthony in a Romanesque Revival style. The church featured traditional details like the bell tower, mixed with modern elements such as the brise-soleil screens over the windows on the first floor. This photo was taken in 1950.

In 1919, Fort Lauderdale charter captain Jimmy Vreeland and his guests reeled in six sailfish. The story goes that pioneer resident M. A. Hortt tied them to his car and drove to Biscayne Park in Miami, attracting an admiring crowd, and sports fishing became all the rage in Fort Lauderdale. In this image, the *Lucky Lady* carries on this historic tradition in the 1950s.

On a sunny day in April 1950, visitors enjoy Fort Lauderdale's golden beach. From left to right are Jean Hubert, Donna Stallings, and Bob Hess, at the time manager of the local chamber of commerce.

After World War II, the city of Fort Lauderdale acquired the former Coast Guard Base 6, located at the south end of the beach. In December 1949 a new marina, Bahia Mar, opened on the site. Bahia Mar put the city on the map in the boating business, as it brought tremendous publicity and cachet to potential investors and new residents. This view shows the shopping center at Bahia Mar about 1950.

Bahia Mar became one of the country's most glamorous yachting marinas, a title it can still claim today. It featured a number of amenities for its guests, many of whom were seasonal visitors (a.k.a. "snowbirds"). This is the nursery school at Bahia Mar in the early 1950s.

This photograph by Charles Barron shows Fort Lauderdale's "strip," viewed south from the Lauderdale Beach Hotel in 1955. The empty lawn at far-right in the background is the lawn of the old Las Olas Inn—formerly located at East Las Olas and Atlantic Boulevard (A1A)—demolished in 1954. Tourists and locals could easily find beachside parking for free back in the 1950s.

The opening of Bahia Mar, the postwar boom, and a burgeoning of boat shows, boat parades, and other maritime attractions fueled the amazing growth of the marine industries in Fort Lauderdale in the 1950s and 1960s. In this 1955 photo, a cabin cruiser shares the water with two sailboats on their way to nearby islands.

Port Everglades has long been a place where African-American workers could hope to find a decent wage, even in the days of Jim Crow and widespread prejudice. Here longshoremen unload cargo from Cuba in this early 1950s image. Commerce with Cuba disappeared after the U.S. severed ties in 1961, following Castro's 1950s violent revolution that established a communist government on the island.

The "Philip Morris bellhop" was a popular American advertising icon of the 1930s, 1940s, and 1950s. The original character, Johnny Roventini, served as an ambassador at countless parades and celebrations throughout the nation. The diminutive Johnny, already over 20 in the 1930s, was backed up by a corps of young imitators. In this photo, one of the "junior Johnnies" visits Fort Lauderdale for a parade or festival in the 1950s.

In the 1950s, drive-in movie theaters provided a popular evening pastime for families and courting couples throughout America. Fort Lauderdale's first drive-in was located at West Broward Boulevard and Northwest Twenty-Seventh Avenue. This east-facing aerial view by local photographer Tony Kozla shows the drive-in, with Broward Boulevard at upper-right.

Fort Lauderdale became the state's fifth-largest city as its population grew from around 35,000 to 83,648 in the 1950s. New homes and housing developments sprang up through every corner of the community. This image features a "cool" ranch house with "midcentury modern" detailing (once considered old-fashioned but now trendy again) at Davie Boulevard and Southwest Seventeenth Avenue. Students pass by on their way to school, some carrying what appear to be sack lunches.

In 1956, longtime residents said farewell to the aging wooden station that had served the Florida East Coast Railway since the beginning of the twentieth century. The new station, opened in June of that year, was located on Southwest Seventeenth Street. It did not serve the public long; by 1968 the FEC would cease passenger service.

Bennett Elementary was constructed at 1755 Northeast Fourteenth Street in 1951, and named for Ulric Bennett, longtime superintendent of county schools. This photo features the students of Mrs. Margaret Morris' sixth-grade classroom in the 1956-57 school year.

In the 1950s, the miles of Fort Lauderdale waterways and the establishment of Bahia Mar attracted an increasing number of "live-aboard" residents like the family shown in this 1957 photo. The community was once known for its houseboats and easy accessibility for pleasure boaters, but city policies have become increasingly restrictive to combat water pollution.

Colonel and Mrs. Robert Wheat and friends enjoy an entirely Florida-style Christmas at their home in 1957. The Wheats lived in a house designed by Fort Lauderdale "environmental" architect Bill Bigoney. Bigoney's house designs focused on the link between exterior and interior spaces, to take advantage of Florida's natural breezes in the days before air conditioning.

In 1957, the completion of the Sunshine State Parkway, a.k.a. the turnpike, signaled a new era for automobile travel in Florida. Originally, the highway linked North Miami with Fort Pierce and had only occasional exits. Here the "Flying L" band of Fort Lauderdale High School performs during dedication ceremonies at the headquarters, located at the Sunrise Boulevard entrance. The speaker is Governor LeRoy Collins.

Although the southern half of the county had largely abandoned farming for real estate and tourism, winter vegetables were still the focus of north Broward's economy in the 1950s. In this 1957 photo, workers near Fort Lauderdale sort the latest pick of bell peppers.

In March 1949, WTVJ (then Channel 4) became the first television station to begin broadcasting from Miami. By the end of the 1950s, a number of others had joined the new industry in South Florida, with limited hours and offerings. Here a live-aboard family enjoys a show on their small set aboard their sailboat, probably berthed at Bahia Mar, in 1957.

The Town and Country Motel was typical of the "mom and pop" hostelries that once dominated the landscape of the tourist town of Fort Lauderdale. The motel opened in the early 1950s on Federal Highway just north of the "gateway," where the highway jogs north from East Sunrise Boulevard. The Town and Country featured apartments as well as motel rooms, a swimming pool, and a great luxury at the time—air conditioning.

During the land boom of the 1920s, local developers Charley Rodes and W. F. Morang began the ambitious task of developing the swampy lands surrounding East Las Olas Boulevard as "islands." Few were finished until after World War II. "Hendricks Isle," Northeast Eighteenth Avenue, was one of the first to be completed north of Las Olas. This view shows the neighborhood, looking north from Las Olas Boulevard in the 1950s.

In 1934, Indian activist and Fort Lauderdale pioneer Ivy Stranahan founded the Friends of the Seminoles as a support organization dedicated to the native peoples who once called the Fort Lauderdale area home. Education was a key program of the Friends, and many Seminole children were sent to receive an education at Cherokee School in North Carolina. In this photo Mrs. Stranahan, Mrs. N. Ritchie Johnson, and Mrs. O. H. Abby receive thanks from Reverend Billy Osceola in 1959.

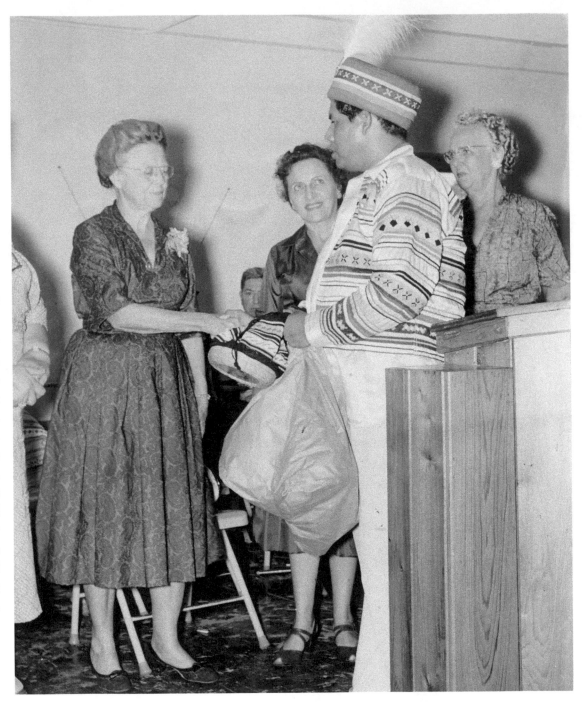

The *Ina B*, out of Cleveland, Ohio, pays a sun-drenched visit to Fort Lauderdale's Intracoastal Waterway in this 1959 scene. Left to right are Lynn Genaria and Mr. and Mrs. T. Warren Smith.

By the early 1960s, Fort Lauderdale's downtown retail district was in decline as the new, suburban shopping centers arose, away from the center of town. This photo features former shopping mecca Andrews Avenue, then still host to many retail establishments. The view faces north from just north of Wall Street (today known as the eastern entrance to Las Olas Riverfront) on the west side of the street.

DECADES OF CHANGES

(1960–1970s)

The Pier 66 marina and hotel complex was the "happening" place in the 1960s for visitors and locals alike. Its beautiful views of the local waterways have long made it a premier meeting facility and convention hotel. It has also employed a good number of local residents, including the cleaning crew shown gathered around a cart on the docks in this 1961 photo by Johnny Johnson.

War Memorial Auditorium opened in Fort Lauderdale's Holiday Park in 1950. It served for many years as the city's only large public venue, home to opera, prize fights, and graduations. In this scene, it plays host to a Democratic Party rally for the 1960 election. Supporters hold placards supporting Dorr Davis for juvenile court judge and Danian A. J. "Red" Ryan, who was reelected to the state legislature in November of that year.

Democrats rally at the War Memorial Auditorium in this October 1960 photo. The posters on the stage showcase the Democratic hopefuls for the presidential campaign, John F. Kennedy and his running mate, Lyndon B. Johnson. Ironically, Broward County went Republican during the November election, casting 68,294 votes for Richard Nixon versus 47,811 for JFK.

In the summer of 1961, the Fort Lauderdale NAACP staged a series of "wade-ins" on Fort Lauderdale beach to force county commissioners to construct a causeway and provide adequate facilities for African-American citizens at the "Negro beach" just south of Port Everglades. The wade-ins definitely captured the attention of the local citizenry, long accustomed to segregated beaches.

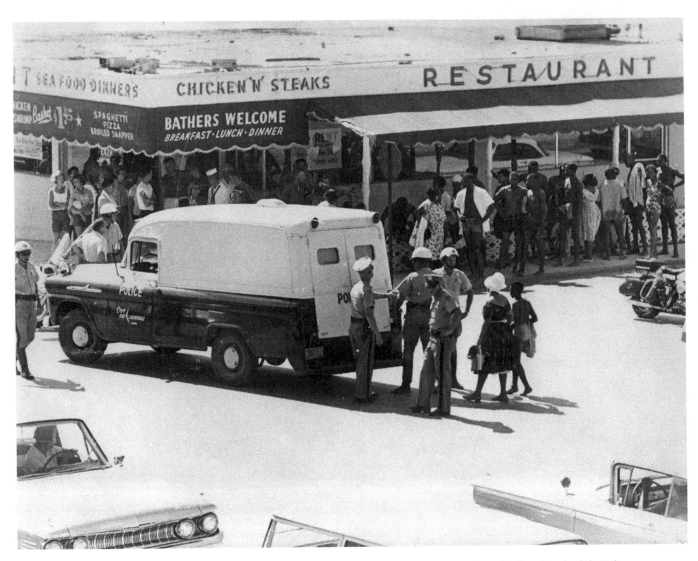

Members of the National Association for the Advancement of Colored People are escorted to the Fort Lauderdale Police Department's paddy wagon at East Las Olas and Almond Avenue during a beach "wade-in" in July 1961. Eula Johnson, NAACP president and wade-in organizer, is visible at right, in the floral hat.

This photo features a panoramic view of New River, looking east from just west of the Andrews Avenue bridge, in the early 1960s. The bridge, shown in operation, is the third version of the span, completed in 1949. In 1979, the current bridge was built, with much longer and higher proportions. The "new" bridge is much more serviceable, but it made North and South New River Drive obsolete and forever altered the view at this historic spot.

The New York Yankees, baseball's most famous team, brought their spring training camp to Fort Lauderdale in 1962 for a 33-year stint. Locals enjoyed watching the Yanks at the newly constructed Fort Lauderdale Stadium (a.k.a. Yankee Stadium) near Executive Airport. Left to right are manager Ralph Houk, Mickey Mantle, Governor Farris Bryant, Roger Maris, and Wendell Jarrad, chair of the Florida Development Commission.

In the 1950s, city leaders actually invited students at colleges throughout the U.S. to make Fort Lauderdale their destination for Easter vacation. Ten thousand students appeared on an annual basis. In December 1960, the movie which fictionalized this phenomenon, *Where the Boys Are,* premiered in Fort Lauderdale. The next spring, locals were aghast when 50,000 students invaded town. Here is a classic Spring Break scene from 1962.

The mild waves of Florida's southeast coast have never been known as a surfing mecca—but the locals are always willing to give it a try, particularly before or after a hurricane. Here an intrepid surfer takes on a wave at Fort Lauderdale's beach in the 1970s.

Three New Zealanders on world tour stop for a snapshot at "the" spot on the strip on Fort Lauderdale's beach in spring of 1962.
At left is the Las Olas Plaza, which replaced the old Las Olas Inn in 1959. At far-right, the world-famous Elbo Room, epicenter
for Spring Break activities, is visible at the corner of A1A and East Las Olas Boulevard.

By the 1960s, the growth of the city's downtown discouraged the charters' use of their traditional docks on New River—the smell of fish was no longer acceptable there. The increased population also began to seriously affect the game fish environment as more boaters impacted more reefs. "Captain Bill" still attracted customers from his berth at Bahia Mar, as shown in this photo taken in 1963.

Westwood Heights Elementary School, located just east of the Melrose Park neighborhood in what was then west of the city limits, was one of many new schools constructed in the county during the late 1950s. This image shows a second-grade classroom at the school in 1963. The open, awning-style windows visible here were widely used in the days before schools were air conditioned.

Three young ladies display the latest in (modest) beach wear on Fort Lauderdale's south beach in 1963. One of the widest beach areas in town, the south beach featured a small parking lot, tables, and barbecue grills and is still a popular spot for picnics and parties.

This aerial view features the northernmost part of Fort Lauderdale's "strip" in 1964. At center is the quirky Jolly Roger Hotel. Originally constructed in 1954, it had a pirate theme that included costumed valets and waiters. It still stands, having since lost its piratic name, one of Fort Lauderdale's best examples of what is now called "midcentury modern" style.

This view, north along A1A, was taken from the landmark Yankee Clipper Hotel in 1967. At right is one of Fort Lauderdale's best beaches, featuring the south beach parking lot. At left is the Bahia Mar Yachting Center.

Fort Lauderdale's first temple, Emanu-El, opened on South Andrews Avenue in 1937, the only Jewish temple between West Palm Beach and Miami. By the late 1960s the congregation had outgrown the original structure. In this photo, temple leaders gather for the symbolic groundbreaking of the new Temple Emanu-El located on West Oakland Park Boulevard in Lauderdale Lakes in May 1967.

Las Olas Boulevard has long been known as Fort Lauderdale's "road to the beach." Immediately east of downtown, small houses and churches lined the road for many years, but in the 1950s, a series of exclusive shops arose, and the area established a reputation as the city's own "Worth Avenue," a reference to the upscale shopping area of Palm Beach. Typical of the Las Olas shops was George Horn Fine Foods, located at 825 East Las Olas Boulevard in this 1967 photo.

In December 1965, the city of Fort Lauderdale opened a new, state-of-the-art swim center on the city's south beach, adjacent the old Fort Lauderdale Casino Pool. In 1968, the International Swimming Hall of Fame opened a new museum on the site, where educational exhibitions highlighted the accomplishments of the aquatic arts. In this photo, a diver takes the plunge off the high dive at the Hall of Fame pool in 1967.

In 1967, tourism was clearly the largest single contributor to Broward County's economy, impacting every resident through the revenues it generated. The main attraction— the miles of public beach. This view reveals a typical Fort Lauderdale day under the coconut palms in 1967.

In the 1960s, the paddlewheel-style *Southern Belle* carried passengers from the Plantation Mansion House on Northeast Thirtieth Street down the Intracoastal to Port Everglades every evening. The entertainment was a wholesome, Gay Nineties–style revue, in the manner of showboats of old.

Originally founded by a group of enthusiasts at the University of Miami campus, the Gold Coast Railroad Museum opened its unique attraction in what is today Snyder Park in 1966. It featured historic rail cars and a ride on an authentic, old-time train pulled by a steam locomotive. In December 1984, the entire complex moved to south Dade County to make way for I-595.

One of Fort Lauderdale's most famous citizens is Chris Evert, world-renowned tennis champion who dominated women's tennis in the 1970s and 1980s. Evert was born in Fort Lauderdale, the daughter of longtime city tennis pro Jimmy Evert, whose innovative programs literally put Fort Lauderdale on the tennis map. Chris won 157 singles titles and was the youngest to rank number one since Maureen Connolly.

Fort Lauderdale's Ocean World marine attraction featured tropical fish, sea lions, birds, otters, and the ever-popular dolphin show, shown here in March 1970. Once surrounded by open space, by the 1990s the site was hemmed in by a new shopping center, hotel, and school. Unable to expand, it closed in 1994.

This view, looking south and west, shows Fort Lauderdale's south beach in 1967. In the background center, the entrance to Port Everglades is just visible. Just to the right of center is the oceanliner-shaped Yankee Clipper Hotel, designed by Miami architect Tony Sherman. The beach at right is one of Fort Lauderdale's most historic spots. It was once the site of one of the original forts of Fort Lauderdale, and later, the House of Refuge lifesaving station.

Notes on the Photographs

These notes, listed by page number, attempt to include all aspects known of the photographs. Each of the photographs is identified by the page number, a title or description, photographer and collection, archive, and call or box number when applicable. Although every attempt was made to collect all data, in some cases complete data may have been unavailable due to the age and condition of some of the photographs and records.